breathe in..

exhale...

...

shadows

of a journal

written by ginny brill

...

dear readers, before you begin...

i know this isn't standard,
but before we start, i have a request:
do not try to find her—
it's time to let it rest.

i know you're curious,
to see the faces behind my words,
but this book is about *me*,
not about getting back at her.

please respect her privacy,
and everyone else's too.
i tried to keep things vague enough
to avoid giving away clues.

if you knew us in person,
keep the names to yourselves.
seriously, guys. i don't need saving—
she's already in her own private hell.

doxxing is illegal, and if it gets back to me,
i'll do whatever's necessary
to protect our families **legally**.

this isn't tongue-in-cheek,
not one of my "many jokes."
i didn't use names for a reason—
if you keep reading, you're giving me your oath.

keep your integrity,
-ginny
(no, this is not a shadow poem—that will make sense in a bit...)

...

the journey

...

breathe in...
exhale...

...

dedications

...

to my readers,

i started the journal, before we began,
a wedding day gift, or just a place my mind ran.
i fell too quick, just friends at first,
i loved her before, those hozier lyrics versed.

a game: cat and mouse—and golden retriever,
the love, the laughter, how much i believed her.
she played her parts, and i truly believed,
all of the promises, she swore to me.

from here on out, you'll see the love on the left, the shadows on the
right.
shadows of memories, saved for our wedding night.
the love shines pure, but is haunted by—
the storm in hindsight, that i survived.

forever my gratitude,
-ginny

to the one who inspired me,

i always wrote you poems and songs,
but didn't know how much would be inspired by things gone
wrong.
it was too much of a shame, to throw out the books,
i started weeks in, without giving them a second look.

thanks for the lessons, inspirations and twists,
some because i knew you,
some you'd never guess came from your grifts:
a home i envisioned we'd share, but still mine.
a friend never met, had not for your crimes.

at the start, a song looped in my car—
you were the risk i thought would go far,
now in my car, a shifted perspective plays
"20 times in a day......but i still tried to stay"

i know how you left, how you chased the storm—
an algorithmic chance in the night, your confession informed.
gone by morning, but i saw the reductions,
of our love, our story; so here are my corrections.

gratitude for your inspiration,
-ginny

to the friend who made us feel like family,

we brought chaos and calm to the very same room,
the holidays crowded; anticipations loomed.
laughter tucked into every spare space—
we were embraced and loved; you all made a place.

you said i was kind, the soft kind of strong.
you saw i was real—you said it all along.
you were a friend who showed up as you,
no filters, no games, just honest and true.

i miss the laughter and chaos of six,
how the joy ran wild, the potions and the sticks.
i kept the photos, we all took altogether,
memories of sleepovers, mishaps, and laughter.

and i never once thought i'd wish so strongly to defend
my truth to someone i once called my friend.
i don't know if you'll ever read this book,
but i don't resent you for taking shelter when her ground shook.

if you ever reached out, i don't know what i'd do—
i'd guard my heart, but give it a chance, too.
the silence she left, wasn't only her own,
it marks time of the friendships that could have grown.

forever in love and friendship,
-ginny

to the silence left behind,

you moved in when the truth fell still,
crept in through cracks and drank your fill.
you tucked yourself in every bed,
and whispered grief inside my head.

little questions, in tiny voices—
you follow—because how do i explain her choices?
where once played giggles, like a song—
left you behind, empty and wrong.

easter was a bit more quiet,
a subtle contrast, but i couldn't deny it
memories that never came to pass
echoed loudly, beyond the laughs

you dressed up grief and wore it well,
and turned my home into a shell.
but silence, babe, you've lost your throne—
this phoenix doesn't stand alone.

so go now, silence, pack and leave—
this house holds fire you can't bare to see.
you were the echos, soft and grave—
but now this home is mine to save.

i've filled your gaps with song and dance,
with joy and love, above circumstance.
you tried to hold me in her ghost—
but i chose joy, and laugh the most.

in reclaimed joy,
-ginny

to my daughter's brief best friend,

you ran like twins through the soft autumn air,
matching in dresses, tangled up hair.
friends by chance, but best friends by choice,
each giggle a promise, each whisper a voice.

you didn't ask why—you knew it was right,
the sleepovers, tea parties, movies at night.
you shared stuffed animals, secrets, and songs,
like you'd been waiting for this all along.

i know you probably ask about where she went,
she does too—i can't express how much you meant
i still keep the drawings, you girls made in the fall,
rainbows, pumpkins, you both with your dolls.

so many photos, i saved on my phone,
memory cards, hearts, carved into stones.
i'll never delete them, my baby's memories
you are loved and missed, sweet _____

don't ever stop laughing,
-ginny

to the carelessness,

she blew through lives with a storm on command,
never once thinking who else wouldn't stand.
friendships, routines, the magic they made—
all crushed by a choice she packaged as brave.

she didn't just leave—she shattered the floor,
left children confused at unopened doors.
my daughter still asks why her friend disappeared,
and i dress it up simply—because the truth would sear.

but pieces remain, and i've started to rebuild—
new memories, with laughter, with love refilled.
we plant new joys in the mud the storm left,
and mostly forget how much we first wept

the pictures remain, and so does the grace—
not hers, but ours; somehow we're okay.
the past can't return, but the future can bloom,
and we'll sweep out the broken she left in our rooms

forever growing,
-ginny

to the boy i will always love as mine,

you were 4, then 5, but you filled the house,
with stomping feet, and a giggle that bounced.
best friends one minute, then throwing a fit—
you and my son, like fire and grit.

you called me "dad-mom" once or twice,
a funny distinction, but a name that felt right.
we shared three lego movies just before the day,
i dropped you off, and this all went away

your drawings always looked like memories—
you sketched the world with care and ease.
your skill surpassing kids your age,
and one of your drawings still dances on its fridge stage.

i miss your voice. i miss your noise.
your monster truck roars, the chaos and toys.
you took your spot beside my kids, in time,
growing like siblings, their stories and mine.

i never got to say goodbye—
just blinked, gone, little explanation why.
but i carry you still, in things we did,
in legos and books, and how fiercely you lived.

wherever you are, i hope you're okay.
i hope you're laughing and finding lucky pennies along the way.
and if you ever wonder, if i still love you—
know there's a "dad-mom" out here whispering: i do.

forever my love,
-ginny

to the lies, manipulation, and phantoms of confessions in the night,

days prior, i was the best ever,
$63 in gas station snacks, not quite a small endeavor.
post-surgery, i could relate
been there, done that; so i took the weight

everything i'd always wished i'd had done,
to help ease your pain, took care of your son.
illness befell our home after 3,
days of recovery, you and him...and also me.

yet i still was the best, for a few more days
caught up in med schedules, fears, and flu haze
but the day i collapsed, you didn't even know
you thought i was mad, thought i was sicker for show

when he struggled to breathe, i wanted to be there
you told me to go home, and pretended i didn't care
i checked in, but you wanted space.
boundaries never crossed, not even to save face

you got spun up in your narratives, wrapped up in deceit,
protection, aggression—but where are the receipts?
you gave your many reasons, carefully crafted to win—
but a thunderstorm is why; you invited him back in.

forever writing,
-ginny

breathe in...
exhale...

...

the first chapter

...

mid-may
before we ever met in person after
a few weeks of texts and phone calls

it feels like something from the start—
a lyric lodged inside my heart.
i can't quite place it, can't quite name—
just know my soul has caught a flame.

you ask the questions that go deep,
the kind that steal a night of sleep.
you laugh too hard, and so do i—
we both forget the reasons why.

i find myself rereading texts,
like somehow they reveal what's next.
you quote that song, my heart it flew—
like we're circling something soft and true.

whatever this becomes, or not,
i'm thankful for this spark i've caught.
i don't know why, i don't know when—
but i feel like i would choose you, now and then.

good thing i didn't burn this journal...

i wrote you down in early may,
in pages i later hoped was for wedding days.
a spark, a smile, a favorite song.
you felt significant; i wasn't wrong.

so much in common; "meant to be"
like blood that ran through arteries.
but darling, if that line was true,
why did i bleed, and why didn't you?

we talked for hours, every night.
i thought it meant our stars aligned
but all those calls and dopamine highs,
were just your habit, not a sign

you made me laugh, you made me glow
but i've built a home you'll never know
i saved those lyrics like sacred proof—
you said them first, but not in truth

so here's some final words to you:
i loved you more than you could do.
and now this pen rewrites the end,
not for a bride—not for a friend.

mid-may
first time meeting in person

i met you quiet, tucked in sleeves,
a little sick, still hard to believe.
a little care-package meant for your door,
met you instead, i manifested it, i swore.

your smile says stay, and something in me does—
i feel a warmth i hadn't because.
we talk easily, like we've already met,
like fate just hadn't introduced us yet.

the car drive home, a song loops thrice,
the stars were bright, the evening so nice
i whisper, "this risk feels worth the fall—"
and sit here with the details i can recall.

i laughed too much, you smiled too wide,
i think you saw that look i couldn't hide.
i wonder if you feel it too—
this quiet thread that leads to you.

i was trying to take care of you before i
even knew you...

you first met me sick, in cardigan and chills,
your arms full of my kindness and gestures.
we talked like old souls, skipping the frills—
you made me feel safe in all measures.

you said the right things without being prompted,
like a wish i forgot i had penned.
and my god, the facades you concocted—
it's like you read my thoughts to pretend.

the song on repeat had barely begun,
but it looped in my head going 'round.
the lyrics said love—i thought you were the one.
but it really wasn't quite that profound.

i whispered, "this risk, i think it's worth taking,"
convinced by your smile and the stars overhead.
but babe, in hindsight, i think i was aching—
not for you, but for the hope that you fed.

mid-may
bees to a flower

you tend to your flora, your touch so divine,
a goddess of nature, planted in my mind.

ocean fire in your eyes, a wild, feral grace
no desire to look away or pull from your embrace.

i crave your knowledge, obsessed with your passions,
every word watering vines of a life i can almost imagine.

honey-dripped whispers, laced with your wit,
drawn like bees to a flower, and i love all of it.

the storm on the horizon

you spoke of bees and garden beds,
seeds hand-sown by words you said.
you showed me love of blooming form—
but hid the looming thunderstorm.

your plants were poems, sweet and green.
your words, like spells—too soft to scream.
i let them root beneath my skin,
not knowing where you'd truly been.

you said you felt it just as deep,
but your love was a wolf, playing sheep.
you mirrored back what i had shown—
then left me in the garden alone.

you said we'd choose us, every day.
you chose yourself. then walked away.
and yet, i bloom. despite the frost.
you weren't the one. you were the cost.

mid-may
ice-cream fairy

sick again, but no big deal
we talk for hours, and i can feel
this building connection, the playlists, the rocks
maybe, just maybe, this will be what i thought.

i brought you some food, dropped off at the door
your son excited to learn who the ice cream was for
"ice cream fairy"—i love how that sounds
i'm excited to watch this grow leaps and bounds.

sometimes i worry, i'm being too much
but you're sending signals, that i'm just enough
invisible strings, tied through the skies
the stars above, a spark in our eyes

ice cream melts quickly...

i wrapped your world in softer care,
while mine unraveled, unaware.
you let me show up, one by one—
the gestures stacking under the sun.

you let me tend, but kept your space,
cat and mouse—you wanted the chase.
i called it fate, i traced your stars—
but wishes can't heal old scars.

i made you playlists, a bracelet too,
you liked the attention, but "real" scared you.
you let me fall, you let me write—
but now my poems will get the spotlight.

mondays are for - almost late may

intrigue, passion, brilliance
authentic, laughter
connection

sundays are for

insight, grounding, clarity
enlightened, silence
becoming

almost late may
you're significant...

incredible, and i know it's fast,
but i would love it, if this connection could last.
you call me kind—it's just my nature:
to nurture, to care, to never denature.

i sort of see a flashing glimpse,
of future dreams we may not want to miss.
we share our dreams—so much the same!
i wouldn't dare to say now, but i could take your name...

i joke, i joke, but maybe not—
no really, too soon—these damn thoughts.
something feels fated, something feels real.
you're significant, that part i feel.

still true...

you called me kind, you called me right—
and still you vanished overnight.
i laid my soul out line by line,
you took my pages and left the spine.

i saw the future in your smile—
planned it out, inch by mile .
you mirrored dreams i didn't fake—
i'd give and give, you'd take and take.

i built a world where i was sure,
but god, your actions were the cure.
it was necessary, the pain and strife—
you were significant, just not my wife.

almost late may
after our ~~first date~~ hanging out

we called it a date, it's best to know.
and we both agreed, we wanted to move slow.
we laughed, we talked, we played a game.
no kiss—just a hug, that sparked a flame.

inside my soul, something stirred.
your eyes to mine, our hearts blurred.
you set aside days, to give us space.
probably a good idea...to pace.

but when you make, my phone awaken,
the image is the string you painted.
you feel it too, and give me signs,
that maybe someday, i'll call you mine.

for now some dates, that end with hugs.
finding rocks, nature, and bugs.
the tarot cards, all point to fate.
i need to stop writing—it's time for our next date.

if you don't get it, google the game

you said the word before that night.
"date" is what you called it,
but over time, that label changed:
a foreshadow into your bullshit.

we laughed, we talked, we felt aligned,
but something in you shifted.
constantly guessing, the game you played:
poetry for neanderthals—hinting?

get...close.......ghooost....
leave...on...read...
i ~~really~~ should...have...knooown.
the time for space, was part of the storm,
not for something grown.

i know you felt it, you couldn't have faked it,
not everything at least.
you gave me crumbs and let me starve,
while enjoying your whole feast.

"i want to start as friends," you said,
and i agreed, 'cause yeah, me too.
not knowing that eventually,
i'd lose your friendship, but you'd lose me too.

late may
a walk in the park

a wooden spoon that i once made,
a symbol of attention paid.
i'll see your cues, and offer mine,
when spoons run out, throughout our climb

you take it and then look at me,
is it the light, or a tear i see?
something we've both been looking for,
i can't wait to get to know you more.

we always hug, at the end of our dates,
i'm trying to hush the thoughts of fate.
i don't know why, but it seems to fit,
that a greater purpose for us, just may exist.

guess we didn't make it out of the rain...

i gave you a spoon and heart-shaped stones,
you gave me dopamine through a phone.
i followed feathers, numbers, songs,
believed the path could not be wrong.

i carved that spoon, you praised the thought—
i never asked what your love cost.
you said my name like it was kind,
but never really let your heart align.

i held you close with care and grace,
but it was just the start of your game of chase.
a greater purpose for us existed,
but i couldn't see it, 'til it'd all been twisted.

late may
darling...

you called me darling, on the phone,
i'm starting to feel not quite alone.
you sent an emoji 🤟, my soul ablaze!
what did she mean? was it a mistake!?

i added some songs silently to,
the playlist we share, songs for you.
a little bit bold, to say how i feel,
through songs and lyrics—it's getting real.

i thought it meant something...

you called me darling, i hit replay—
made myself bold, the very next day.
i sent you songs, you sent a sign,
and i believed you mirrored mine.

but now i see the way you took—
but gave me material for this book.
and what felt warm, was just a hue—
you weren't in love, you liked the view.

late may
~~*second date*~~ *hanging out*

told me to stop looking at you like that,
but my face was responding in kind.
those ocean eyes bore into me.
i swore they were saying, "mine."

sometimes i sense, i say too much....
reveal my thoughts unsaid.
sending poems, and adding songs,
while texting you from bed.

and i must admit, sometimes i wonder.
what you do those days,
the days where you take that time for yourself
and my ringer doesn't play.

but i also know that i'm intense,
i feel things deep and true.
i'll slow down, not send *all* the poems.
i just know, i want to know you.

our "real" 2nd date later was a restaurant
she didn't remember me taking her to...

you looked away when i reached near—
and i mistook your pause for fear.
i wrote it off, rewrote the signs,
ignored the shadow, in your lines.

i pulled back words, i meant to say,
afraid i might have pushed you away.
you weren't confused—just playing soft,
while holding hands you hadn't dropped.

i saw the shift, but rewrote the scene,
asked myself "what did she mean?"
i stayed your friend, behind a smile,
okay with love taking a while.

you made me question what was true—
while hiding him, and hiding you.
and now i see what you concealed:
thunder crashes—you never healed.

late may
you almost said it way before i did...

wildflowers
banana bread,
poems swirling
in my head

you almost said
something tonight.
a slip, we laughed
but it still feels right.

brief visit, two hugs, budding inspiration—
words flowing—
a sort of knowing,
not an imposition.

sometimes it feels
like chasing the wind,
but i will *not*...
let my insecurities win.

you say a lot of things though...

i offered poems,
and clovered days.
i gave you hope,
in gentle ways.

you almost said it,
then took it back.
you danced in comfort,
and i kept track.

a slip of tongue,
a softened smile—
you let me hang,
for quite a while.

i picked the flowers,
you kept the vase.
a fleeting stop,
on your way some...place.

late may
ever wake up to texts sent in the
shadows of the night?

a few days ago we talked—again—
another conversation about us just being friends
"i don't think so..." you said on the phone,
but those texts scream "yes"...maybe my feelings aren't alone??

my heart was racing, this morning when i woke.
and saw the missed call and... *holy smoke*...
the one stinkin' night, my phone was on vibrate.
probably for the best, remember, you're pretending to be *straight* ;-)

or maybe you've actually decided to not care,
about what your family thinks, because you can see something rare.
friends don't say what you said to me,
but i know i need to navigate this carefully...

i'm so glad my phone was on silent...

"let's go slow,"
you softly said,
then dreamt me up with words,
you wanted to unsend.

you ghosted, flirted,
push, retract—
your words always sweet,
'til you took them back.

you said you shook,
you wished me near,
but couldn't escape
your maze of fear.

so next time someone
calls me kind—
i have new lessons,
to keep in mind.

late may
so many green beans...

we planted beans,
in cups of plastic.
you planted hope
it was fantastic.

too bad they mostly died...

string beans in cups,
lined in a row.
you let them wither—
like much you sow.

-Beanageddon 2024

early june
sometimes...

sometimes,
things just work.

and then sometimes...

sometimes,
it's not how we expect.

early june
anything else is a lie

you called me an angel,
it made my heart kind of skip.
each smile in my direction,
sends my soul on a trip.

your laughter brings me joy—
a joy i can't describe.
a joy that makes a home.
a joy that makes me feel alive!

your hand grazes casually,
with anyone else, not a thought.
but there's something about you—
my heart is hopelessly caught.

your smile, your heart,
your mind, your words.
i vow to make sure:
you always feel heard.

everything about you,
sends me to cloud 9.
cliché? maybe.
but anything else is a lie.

something else was the truth

you called me an angel,
and maybe i was.
but wings don't mean much,
when flying comes with a clause.

your laughter was music,
it felt like home.
but silence echoed loudly,
when i tried to be known.

your touch felt like magic—
until it grew cold—
and i clung to the stories—
to the lies that you told.

your smile, your spark,
your carefully chosen tone—
i mistook the attention,
for you wanting to build a home.

everything about you—
once felt like proof.
but now i see clearly—
something else is the truth.

early june
things were quiet...

it's been a few days,
some 1-on-1 with your kid.
but even in your absence,
i'm struggling to keep these feelings hid.

then we hang out,
and so do the boys,
"...almost like brothers..."
you whisper, as they share toys.

oh, my heart leapt!
this feels so fated.
i think you're starting to drop the worries,
of your family and someone you once dated

but i was learning that was the pattern...

you said our sons,
could be like brothers—
but you can't fake fate,
and replace others.

you spoke of strings,
a cosmic thread—
i made plans,
while you misled.

you said "best friend,"
you meant a phase—
while i was busy,
paying your way.

early june
can you uber anymore...
without thinking about me?

ubering with you,
is not a chore.
it's something worth the gasoline—
to do more.

because time with you,
is time standing still.
take your time,
because this is real.

i care so much,
want you to see.
just how much,
you already mean to me.

probably not...

i held your world,
with tender grip.
and let you choose,
how close we'd sit.

you called me kind,
you called me real—
but never dared,
to truly feel.

i'd wait, i'd build,
i'd plant with pride—
while you kept him,
just to the side.

early june
take my phone off silent
(the foreshadowing in this poem is wild, because i wrote it back in june)

i take my phone off silent,
solely just for you.
to miss any of your calls,
is not something i want to do.

you invade my mind, frequently.
your vines sending roots deep—
twisting into all of my thoughts,
creating dreams i wish to keep.

if you think you aren't pretty—
you're right—because you're stunning.
in the traditional sense, of course,
but deeper—your mind is truly something!

you're so intelligent and funny,
i'll admit you're funnier than me.
hanging on as words dance off your lips,
and hoping you'll let me listen, endlessly.

sometimes, i forget to breathe,
locked gaze, mesmerized by your eyes.
wondering if i circle your thoughts too,
or if i'm telling myself pretty little lies.

your notifications are muted now

i used to wait in silence—
phone bright against the blue—
as if a call could sort out,
the thoughts i sifted through.

you lingered in the corners,
your vines grew to fill my mind—
but not in ways that blossom,
just tangled in rocks and time.

you called me an angel,
but only when i'd bend—
when shining meant not speaking,
when giving had no end.

you made the world feel weightless,
your stories wrapped in gold—
but laughter isn't safety,
and warmth can still be cold.

i used to hold my breath then,
lost deep in ocean eyes—
not sure if you had seen me,
or just liked how i'd rise.

and now i keep things quiet,
not waiting for a sound—
there's peace in finally breathing,
when no one else is around.

approaching mid-june
a day at the park

the river flooded, like my mind,
watching logs, just drift on by.
digging up flowers, building bug huts
i can feel it, down in my gut

the kids laugh so much,
playing together,
the giggles that came from
all that rainy weather.

your son—he is requesting me now—
not someone else—but *my* house.
i can't wait to teach him the cool stuff i know.
i played him guitar already while babysitting, though!

you're starting to whisper to my heart,
in ways i wanted to manifest.
but i'm a believer in freewill,
so my job is to simply rest.

in hindsight the flooding was excellent foreshadowing

i showed your son the way to love,
and thought you'd see what i was made of.
but legacy means nothing much,
to those who lie with every touch.

we built a world in garden soil,
with children laughing through the toil.
you said the roots were growing too—
but only mine were made for two.

you let your son say i was right—
the one he hoped would stay at night.
but you were torn, and so was he—
you played with hearts too carelessly.

you smiled when i believed in fate,
while whispering to hearts i'd hate.
and still i stayed, too blind to see,
you weren't growing things with me.

mid-june
"i adore you"

"i adore you"

looping in my mind
only you, everything else
vanquished out of sight
everything i do now

you're woven in my thoughts
ones my face can not hide
universal clues that i adore you, lots

that's not what she meant

no more stories circling
over 'n' over in my head
the words laced with shadows

and, "is that what she meant?"
never was a steady flame
you flickered, once or twice
my heart tried to shelter it
only to pay the price
real love wouldn't hide like that
every time i spoke my truth

bent myself to make it last
all you offered was excuse
broken, then blooming–funny how that goes
empowered now. unstoppable. i hope the silence shows

mid-june
it's nice to have a friend

it's nice to have a friend
climbing treehouse ladders
while spinning
into clouds
of lavender fields

it's nice to have a friend
running through purple
and yellow seas of flowers
screaming ferociously
with wind whipped hair

it's nice to have a friend
when it's time to go home
and you need a spare hairpin
to tuck those feral tendrils
back into your woven braids

it's nice to have a friend
when the day is dark
and you need some light
but really
it's nice to have a friend
like you

i keep my circle smaller now

you were my best friend
climbing ladders you watched me build
only to laugh
when i fell
through the clouds

you were my best friend
until you sprinted ahead
through flowers i planted
leaving silence
in your wake

you were my best friend
letting me unravel
while you held the pins
that could've
kept me whole

you were my best friend
but when the dark came
you left me to be
my own light
and really
you weren't my friend at all

mid-june
like a drug

like a drug
swirling in my mind
altering my thoughts to be
cloud 9
drifting below
above it
there's only you

good thing i don't do drugs

like a drug
you held me close
in dreams that begged for us
we fell from grace
i miss the rush
but not at the cost
of you

mid-june
grey & yellow

grey and yellow,
swirling 'round.
perfect balance,
equilibrium found.

when things are heavy,
i can lift.
when the kitchen drawer's empty,
i'll sense the shift.

crossed paths,
invisible strings,
a familiar friendship–
my end to the means.

i'll always have a spoon—
a charger, or a hug.
hand me the cord,
i have the plug.

golden retriever,
and black cat,
quite the perfect pair—
it's a matter of fact.

yellow shines brighter alone

grey seeped slowly,
into yellow bright.
til light grew dim,
in your endless night.

i held your weight—
you let me strain.
you drained my sun—
then cursed the rain!

you took my light.
you praised my glow.
then left me dim,
with none to show.

those strings we swore,
had held us tight—
you cut yours loose—
i called *that* right.

golden retriever,
steady and still.
black cat ran,
to chase her will.

mid-june
signs

a lime green car
zipping amongst
the sea of grey concrete
222-2222—
a billboard screams...
a four-leaf clover—
bank logo subliminal messaging
2:22...
the clock changes
ask and you shall receive
signs unnoticed by the masses

still meant for me...

a lime green car
zipping by, and then another...
no longer scanning for her shadow
107777—
my odometer flashes
...7777...
a feather drifts—
alone, softly landing
a lesson wrapped gently in gifts
the number changes
i did too
ask and you shall receive
signs, clear as ever—
meant for me all along

mid-june
the knock...and three-way-call.

we're hanging out,
it's going awesome.
you're excited to go camping—
we're laughing about something about an opossum...

the knock was firm,
but sort of gentle.
your eyes flashed and i knew,
who was storming the temple.

the drama he's causing—
i'm so freaking sorry.
of course i don't mind,
helping you correct the story!

it's a hilarious twist,
a three-way call—
like we're kids again,
gossiping in the hall!

i promise to you,
my support is no big deal!
i know it hurts that,
they didn't consider how you'd feel.

and now you have the bracelet,
"bff babes for life"
i'm here because i'm your friend,
though i admit i still hope my future...

yes, you guys can groan at me
for brushing this off...

the knock came soft,
but i knew the sound—
your other life
still hanging around.

you had me stay inside—
a lie—
"it was nothing,"
but i saw your eyes.

i stayed in that room,
i stayed in the dark—
believing you'd
extinguish his spark.

but you kept both,
and smiled sweet—
and i mistook it,
for feeling deep.

you had me confess that
it was platonic—
on a three-way call.
how. fucking. ironic.

you let him in,
while holding me near.
and told yourself,
you were being clear.

late june
i mean, it should have been a clue...

i still think it was weird,
the crazy, funny story.
a call with your ex,
defending your glory.

i'm sorry our friendship,
is being weaponized.
but i hate that i omitted the feelings,
i feel linger behind our eyes.

he says his intentions,
are only your son.
but i think it's more.
he thinks you're "the one."

reassured by your words,
and signs i begged for,
gifts from the universe;
the leaves of four.

we're taking our time,
and getting to know,
the souls behind,
the masks that we show.

i still wish you the best of luck!

i gave you luck,
and so much time,
a stone etched deep
with love's design.

you hugged me, sure,
but looked right through—
because somewhere else,
he waited too.

you let me wait,
you watched me try,
you said just enough
but left out the lies.

that three-way call,
felt weird and wrong,
lies through omission—
like we didn't have songs.

and every "thank you"
wore a mask—
the silent truth,
to what he'd asked.

approaching late june
the daily poems were your idea...

i haven't written,
in a few days.
you "can't see us"
i kinda feel played...

then again, social cues—
they're hard for me.
it's possible i was only seeing,
what i wanted to see...

you do flirt though—
my friends say i'm not crazy.
but also this is weird territory,
and with women, things can be hazy.

that poem i wrote,
i keep kicking myself...
i am really worried i blew,
our friendship to hell.

i think i got bold,
with our poetry routine.
and misread some signs,
in the ones you sent me.

friends don't exchange nightly poems...
well, sometimes friends do, but this
time for opinions for a book...

i spoke the truth,
you played pretend—
fed me a spark,
then called it "just friends."

i gave you my poem,
like we did nightly—
then you doused the flame,
or was that, "letting me down lightly?"

i gave you my heart,
you gave me the cold—
said "you don't see us,"
but you still let it unfold.

you knew what i felt,
you read every line—
and still you let silence,
pretend you were kind.

but that poem? it's power.
it lives on without you.
it was never a question—
you just feared the truth.

approaching late june
the one that destroyed everything...

it's visceral–
i can't explain it.
this invisible,
emotional
connection...

when things shift
out of balance
for you–
it shakes
my world now, too...

twisted strands.
entwined vines.
you—
entangled in my heart,
invading my mind...

i welcome you in,
please stay in my life!
best friends for always,
and maybe someday
if i'm lucky—-
well, ah, where was i—

i won't try to guess,
what the future holds...
i love the strings,
that connect us.
and knowing you,
is enough....

it was never the poem...
shadow poem originally written in late june after the previous poem
was delivered

shattered heart,
like glass splintered all around.
one minute cloud 9–
the next...
on the ground.

two flames burn together,
but also apart.
destined to chase...
to run away...
so far...

i'm devastated to know,
we'll lose key parts of life.
not watching this grow–
cuts.
like. a. fucking. knife.

i would have done anything.
i would have moved the stars.
i wanted to choose you daily.
i wanted to tend...
your scars.

i won't try to guess now,
what the future holds...
no longer held by the strings,
that i wove with you...
in gold.

late june
she still wants to be friends...

i really thought, i had blown,
the shot to keep our friendship.
i'm not entitled to explanations—
boundaries accepted.

there's still a shred of hope, i just can't shake...
probably, "...free will..."
regardless, your friendship is enough—
i'll get over how i feel.

(i know how it sounds, guys...)

you didn't choose me—just the high,
a hit of care to get you by.
you kept me close, but out of reach,
then blamed my depth, called it a breach.

you said "best friend," but that was thin—
you meant "stay near, don't let me sin."
but i was more than your escape—
i was the truth you couldn't take.

mid-july
this one was big...

it's been a while since i wrote,
but *everything has changed...*
there's blurred lines, but we discussed it—
and...you didn't look at me the same.

in the best way, i can finally see,
staring through your ocean eyes.
you also feel the way i do,
you finally dropped the disguise!

my face revealed so much more,
than i had ever meant.
you took photos of me with my kid, while looking at you,
then this is how it went...

....
....
....
....

....
....
....
....

quite the story, don't you think?!
like it was written in the stars!
still friends, but friends in...love?
i think i saw beyond your scars...

original interrupted entry, "...nevermind"

we swore it wouldn't change a thing—
but playing with fire can burn and sting.
you knew my feelings from my eyes,
and i mistook that, for the "why"

i asked, "what happens if we fall?"
i knew for me, it meant "freefall"
you said to me, we'd still be friends—
friends in love. no big. the end.

you held my gaze, a second too long,
and we said nothing, but felt the song.
the air was thick with maybe this—
a borrowed truth, a stolen kiss.

we promised light, but struck too loud—
a spark that leapt beyond the vow.
the room went quiet, but not the air,
we crossed a line by staying there.

then you pulled back, once again
to stop your feelings, you must refrain
but when we crossed that hazy line,
you called it nothing—i guess it's fine.

late july
"she's thinking she may want to try again"

"you look at me like you love me,
and write me notes like that..."
words i just wrote down
because you want him back

why am i even still writing?
maybe it's really for me.
i swear i'm happy to just be your friend—
but god this fucking stings.

you literally say you love me—
i just don't say it back.
because i know you mean friends...
but the sting from that slap...

you want me to try to meet someone...
i think maybe someone was flirting...
but i'm not really dating right now—
not for you, but because i'm hurting.

is it because you thought i'd move on?

you wrote me notes,
with glittered light—
"this is your time,"
"you'll shine so bright."

you signed your name,
with loops and love.
said i'd do great,
i was enough.

you told him "i love you"
on the same damn day!
that you hugged me like,
you had meant to stay.

brushed off as old habit,
i hear habits die hard.
feigned distress from your slip,
i let it go with no regard.

beginning of august
you later said you meant to keep it...
but i have my doubts

a little scrap of "trash",
fell out of your purse...
i hope you meant to keep it,
but the alternate is worse.

i wrote on the back,
well, obviously—you can see.
just a fun sticker...haha..
between you and me...

but i'm really very crushed,
you've told me what you want...
you want to be with him,
and "best-friend" is my spot.

i wish i hadn't burned that sticker back now...

you kept the scrap,
most don't keep—
words i wrote,
when i let my heart speak.

a certain look,
that Jim-and-Pam,
i thought it meant,
you gave a damn.

but you said his name,
you chose that storm.
and once again,
you closed my door.

a week later...
HE BLEW IT!!!

you laughed like i was funny again—
you said that you were done with men.
you let me in, and let me be—
and that, alone, was everything to me.

if we never get a shot at more,
i'm still okay with this "before"
you, beside me, stars overhead—
a maybe-love that goes unsaid.

you said he stormed and never stayed.
that thunder always found a way,
to charm you back, then leave you soaked—
you blamed the sky, but never broke—

until that night, you shut the door!
no storm to chase, no need for more.
no crash of thunder just a glow—
a quiet place to finally grow.

oof, let's keep going...

the night was soft,
your voice was warm—
but only lasted,
for as long as you could perform.

it sparked the light,
and i felt seen—
but shadows lingered,
in spaces between.

i didn't know,
you'd recall the storm—
that comfort, for you,
is chaos, of sorts.

early august
"...you knew what it was..."

you wrote the words,
"you're my best friend"—
and we both know,
how that lyric ends.

i hold that line,
like a sacred vow.
you scrawled "i love you,"
and might have meant it...somehow.

but no shared interests or anything...

you knew the lyrics,
but know the real story—
different, but still lies told,
to keep the glory.

but you let me think,
they might be real—
and for a while,
you pretended to feel.

breathe in..
exhale...

...

the second chapter

...

mid-august
the beginning, hozier concert 2024
aka the first "real" date...that i didn't know
was a date

you kiss me like you've known for years,
not just through summer tangled fears.
you hold my hand, say "this is right,"
and all my doubts slip out of sight.

you say you're home when you're with me,
we dream out loud so easily.
we fix things, laugh, we build, we mend—
you're not my start, you're just my when.

we call it fate, we call it choice—
but either way, i love your voice.
and every plan, both wild and true,
starts and ends with me and you.

your ocean eyes, they see me whole—
not just a stop, your end goal.
you promise love, you promise time—
and for the first time, both are mine.

i never would have made a move, since
you said you only wanted to be "friends"

you kissed me like you meant to stay,
but after time you slipped away.
you said it loud—you left me when,
you told your storm "hello" again.

we lit a match, but you summoned in a storm—
you were my future, just not forevermore.
i said "forever," you did too—
but you were the one who asked the storm to take you...

you promised time, you swore it true—
but words you say, don't mean much to you.
love letters and drawings—folded up lies,
promises broken, when you said you "couldn't" even try.

you promised peace, but left a war—
i sometimes still ponder what it was all for.
you took my light, you knew the cost—
but now i shine brighter, i melted your frost

approaching late-august
the early days

you walk through the door, and the air feels right,
like the stars all shifted to shine more bright.
we laugh in my kitchen, you sing while we clean—
and suddenly life feels right and serene.

i didn't plan to fall so deep,
but this kind of love is the kind i keep.
we dance through days that feel brand new—
and every small thing says, "this is true."

we didn't rush, but somehow, fast—
i see forever, i see it can last.
your son's in the hallway, laughing with mine—
and suddenly all of our stars align.

feels a lifetime away now

you walked out the door, and the air turned cold,
stars burned out, future stories left untold.
i still clean the kitchen where we used to laugh—
but now silence cuts the joy in half.

i didn't know it could hurt so bad,
swept back in the storm—it stings and it's sad.
you danced through days like nothing was wrong—
while i sang a future in every song.

maybe we rushed, maybe it came cracked—
i saw forever, but then you didn't look back.
maybe the pace was never the sin,
maybe you just wouldn't let me in.

you said it was for him, you framed it as care—
but love doesn't vanish overnight 'cause you're scared.
he was safe and loved, that part you could feel—
so was it his needs... or your insecurities concealed?

late august
our second "real" date

you lean in, and the night pulls tight,
your lips on mine, the world feels right.
this date, no photos, but i still save,
the way you kissed me—how love behaves.

we took no pictures, but your hands traced,
a memory i carry in every space.
date number two, and i already know—
i want every day to see how this grows.

we did eat there...both had stomach aches after.
i journaled about it even though she later forgot.

we sat close, and we let it be,
no camera roll, just you and me.
i thought that meant we were present and real—
now i see how illusion can steal.

there's nothing to delete, no scene to erase,
no hard proof of that italian-dinner date.
and strangely, i breathe easier that way—
less to grieve now that your love didn't stay.

early september
his birthday...

gifts hidden, scattered around the house,
watching his face light up, scurrying like a mouse.
the table set, for a birthday feast,
a celebration that feels warm and sweet.

a dollhouse gift, it's a big one.
the one found online, just for your son.
the video of him, seeing his surprise—
fills me with love, his joy is the prize.

we ran through the zoo, so much to see—
the squeals and shrieks, giving life to me.
sleepover with your cousin, laughter so loud,
the girls scolded us, to keep the noise down.

then the carnival night, lights all aglow,
i got hit in the face by a teacher, though!
a funny memory, apologies abundant,
for us a new joke, that won't feel redundant.

i really did cherish my memories with him

we had gifts hidden, laughter loud,
but sometimes storms still come with clouds.
we set the table, turned up the lights,
we truly had the best night.

your son lit up, my daughter shrieked,
but underneath, the cracks had seeped.
we ran through zoos, we laughed 'til we cried,
but i missed the worry in your eyes.

i caught a stray punch at the carnival night,
and it was just a funny fright.
and bruises heal faster than trust took to break—
but i'd take that hit, over this ache.

we built a world that felt so right,
but storms were brewing out of sight.
i miss the noise, i miss our light—
but mostly i miss our kids each night.

post mid-september
your birthday-eve

you've made me feel more loved, more known,
than i can convey, in the poems i've thrown.
your laughter settles into my chest,
like every fear has been addressed.

i used to guard my heart so tight,
but now it opens overnight.
not just a partner—you're my best friend,
and i can't wait for what's around the bend.

i see the future in tiny things,
like shared routines and matching rings.
tomorrow, i'll find you birthday blooms—
and set out all the gifts, i'm hiding in my room.

i wonder if this year will beat your "best ever"

we were still good, your touch was gold,
you said forever and my heart was sold.
and i, naive in all my grace,
believed your promises... to stay.

we shared routines and future days,
built quiet joy in the simplest ways.
i never saw the subtle bend,
the path where you'd begin your end.

i planned a birthday, full of delight,
not knowing you'd someday choose flight.
i'd still do it all—just the same—
before the leaving, before your games.

post mid-september
your birthday...

your hands did shake, your voice was low,
when you ask the woman who raised me so—
if forever is something she'd hand to you,
because i'm the one you want to vow to.

and me? i'm asking your cousin too,
if she sees this path the way we do.
she smiles and says she's never seen
you at such peace—so happy, so seen.

we celebrate you with brownies and light,
dinner, arcades, and games all night.
we walk hand in hand down quiet streets,
and i memorize the sound of your feet.

your laugh folds into my walls like glue—
like everything broken now blooms into new.
you make me feel safe, so deeply adored,
like i'm someone you've always waited for.

no rings yet, but we already know—
this love is the kind that dares to grow.
and i can't wait to build what comes next,
with open hands, with hearts unvexed.

my mom has rescinded her blessings

you made your vows before the rings—
asked my mom, said all the right things.
she welcomed you, arms wide and warm—
before she knew you'd chase the storm.

your cousin cheered, said, "this is it,"
but now just nods while you counterfeit.
i lost two women the day you fled—
the one who loved me, and a friend, misled.

you said it yourself—it was the best one yet,
a birthday with not a drip of regret.
i held your joy like it was mine to tend,
not knowing the storm lurked behind the bend.

we celebrated you, i gave you my all—
brownies, the light, and a softened fall.
you held my hand like it meant a vow,
but none of it matters to you now.

the way you beamed, it still haunts me—
like i gave you the version you longed to be.
you said that i felt like coming home,
then left with the storm for me to grieve alone.

no rings anymore, just abandoned plans—
a future unraveled by your own hands.
i dreamt of building, you dreamt of escape—
you burned the blueprints, then burned the landscape.

post mid-september
~~your old bachelorette trip weekend~~
trio-trip with your cousin

we race the swings, we own the day,
a rainbow town of painted rays.
you spin and laugh, you pull me near,
the whole sky tilts down to hear.

pictures snap and colors stir,
your smile caught inside my blur.
we snap each other, flashing grins,
three kids disguised in grown-up skins.

a mishap sprays across the scene,
but even that feels like a dream.
three's a crowd? no fucking way!
i don't know if i've ever laughed more since that day!

the city hums beneath our feet,
already stitching where hearts will meet.

i won't have to rewrite memories,
because they're all part of my story.

we raced the swings, we stole the day,
the city dressed in bright decay.
you laughed and spun and pulled me near,
rewriting what you brought here.

pictures snapped, we froze mid-laugh,
three kids pretending it would last.
the cracks ran under the rainbow stairs,
but god, i only saw you there.

the mishap sprayed, we roared with glee,
i'll recount the story very carefully—
they had to run out—i needed to pay—
ah—nevermind, you had to of been there that day.

drag queens blurred, the neon cried,
a stranger clung, we rode, you smiled.
i missed the signs, i missed the clues—
still too busy falling into you.

but that's on me. i called it fate too soon—
i thought we rewrote all your old wounds.

early october
walks in the park and crafts

we wander the park, kids in tow,
laughing, talking, letting time go.
hand in hand, we roam the streets,
the catching game, with gyms to defeat.

that trip to the river, when you caught that fish,
i captured those memories so they wouldn't be missed.
the water, the laughter, and all of the joy,
making memories, even when it's just us and your boy.

the doormat we paint with our feet side by side,
decorating for halloween—you as my guide.
we take your son out, fun in the night.
trick-or-treating, hearts soaring in flight.

september and october, days full of grace,
with you by my side, i've found my place.
each memory with you, a treasure i write,
a gift for you, to read on our wedding night.

those sure were fun times

we wandered the park, kids in tow,
the laughter and talks, where did it go?
hand in hand, the streets we roamed,
our game—our excuse to leave home.

that trip to the river, when you caught that fish,
i thought those memories fit a perfect wish.
but time has passed, and they slip away...
the river keeps flowing at the end of day...

we painted the doormat, feet side by side.
seven little ghosts, ironic, in hindsight.
now it sits forgotten, haunted memories on the ground.
a ghost of silence, where there used to be sound.

i'll publish these words, once meant for you.
keep telling the story of what i went through:
the love, the excitement, buying ~~our~~ *my* house,
the early games of your cat and mouse...

nearing mid-october
finding ~~our~~ my house

we wandered through empty rooms and felt
a kind of luck unexpected, the perfect hand dealt.
we'll move the lamps, rugs, and hues—
combining lives, forever with you.

i'll never say it's mine alone,
your name is etched into the stones.
we pack your things, i plan your place—
and fill with love, the open space.

your son runs with mine in my dreams,
the kitchen floods with rainbow beams.
i buy this house but plant a vow—
we'll live as one, starting from now.

the sky explodes in swirling light,
a curtain torn across the night.
the northern fire burns above—
the sky itself confirms this love.

it was always meant to be—for me

we had walked through each room and smiled,
the kind of joy that felt so wild.
i signed the deed with love and thrill—
you touched the walls but stayed so still.

your son and mine, they played as kin,
a life we had just started settling in.
i didn't see the warning signs—
the way you froze at being mine.

i told myself all was right,
you smiled, but i sensed the stormy flight.
i repacked your things, your broken vows,
but you're still everywhere, in the shed, even now.

the night sky bled in streaks of flame,
back then, i swore you felt the same.
but what i called a sacred sign—
was just the stars, not some design.

late october
halloween is for laughter

skeleton costumes pinned loose and wild,
we kneel and race like some lost child.
scooby's paws slap down the street,
glow bones cracking beneath our feet.

your laugh lifts higher than the moon,
the whole night feels like a glowing cartoon.
neighbors stare, the stars lean in,
i never want these memories to end.

masks are for halloween

we pinned and knelt and played pretend,
two skeletons racing a night to its end.
you laughed, and god, i loved that sound—
even as the storm shook underground.

that year no kids of mine, just dreams on loan,
thinking of the joy that he's always home.
i ran and laughed and lost that bet,
haunted now by what i can't forget...

early november
the day-to-day...

you text me, "ugh," from down the hall,
and i smile 'cause i know that call.
you cook, i clean, the kids throw rice—
and still, this life feels right and nice.

we bicker small, then laugh out loud,
we're building dreams we plan to vow.
and even tired, stressed, or late—
we hold the line and call it fate.

at first apologies were mutual...

we had started bickering a bit some days,
but it didn't yet overshadow the laughter and play.
the house still held our plans to merge,
but i fear your path was starting to diverge.

i told myself it was just a phase,
not knowing you were shifting ways.
the shift started so early; you said we were fine,
and i trusted your words—your soul's promises to mine.

post mid-november
post-move

moving's tough; this one was hard,
but now we're here, this home, this yard.
the world outside feels bleak and rough,
but here with you, is just enough.

you share the thoughts that once weren't safe,
and know i always come with grace.
and i'm still learning how to deliver,
the kind of love you need to surrender.

you talk to me when my thoughts get loud,
you remind me i shine through clouds.
you love me through the worst i show,
and still believe in where we'll go.

we don't have much, but what we do:
is real, and strong, and always true.
and even now, through stress and strain,
i'd choose this love again and again.

and now my shed is full of packed boxes again

we made it through the move, the mess,
but something started feeling—less.
less joy, less warmth, less eye-to-eye.
i wanted to talk. you didn't like that i cry.

you let me in—or said you did—
but kept a part of you well hid.
i worked so hard to be enough,
while you grew distant, sighed and bluffed.

i begged myself to just believe,
but noted the implied threats to leave.
you promised the opposite: of home, of care—
but some part of you was never there.

i thought our love could face the strain,
could ride the waves, danced in the rain.
but some storms don't announce their break,
they build in silence—then they take.

late november
thanksgiving

holidays,
are not quite the same—
there's so much more joy!
a new magic to name!

your family embraced me,
and embraced all the kids.
(the side that really matters—
where we don't have to stay hid.)

i am so damn thankful for these memories—
the ones from now and later.
it seems like now we're never home,
but i can think of nothing greater!

i love this life with you so much—
one i wasn't sure i'd get to live.
one of many holidays,
we'll make memories that outlive.

one of the things i'll miss the most

holidays,
felt too good to lose,
a favorite? i thought we'd have
forever to choose.

your family embraced me,
i thought you did too—
as we filled the rooms,
in rainbow hues!

i was so damn thankful,
dreaming long and wide—
never seeing just. how. much.
you would hide.

i loved the life i thought we'd hold—
chairs filled, stories spun—
but you left me here,
like it was a table for one.

almost mid-december
"...tomorrow you become my fiancée!"

you had the pen before i knew,
already scripting what we would do.
but i picked up my page and then i said,
"let's both write this chapter up ahead."

now we both have plans tucked out of sight,
both to propose, tomorrow night!
you dreamt of how to make me glow—
i'll raise your bet, show you what i know.

a kollmanii is part of my plan—
a symbol only we understand.
you planned your magic, i planted mine too!
i'm starting this chapter—writing it with you.

see? not poem 33 anymore, but that's okay...

as i write this, it's poem 33...
it won't be once published, but that detail is significant to me.
one more day; i couldn't wait,
to offer my love, to seal our fate.

you had no idea, the surprises i'd planned,
no idea it was more than me asking your hand.
i had planned so much, hell, i didn't stop—
i used every little thing as excuse for a gift-op!

i thought we were writing this chapter together—
i didn't think you could still get caught up in the weather!
i loved you dearly...i probably still do...
but that will fade, when i close this book of you.

mid-december
the proposal

we walk like kids, unsure and wild,
giggles, whispers, our outfits styled.
your fingers twitch, your breath is thin—
nervous, but sure, as this journey begins.

the strings start—our story played,
you kneel, and the noise just fades away.
you say the words that split me whole—
and love takes root inside my soul.

then i kneel too, the picture clear—
the ring, violinist, photographer near.
i speak the words i've always known—
and tell you about the kollmanii for home.

your son, your name, your every tear—
i'll fight to hold, protect, revere.
this isn't just a vow i do—
it's my promise to commit to you.

nobody knew you better...

"no!" you screamed, "i had no idea!"
not meaning the proposal, but surprises revealed.
i had no idea the first thing you'd do,
was sell the promise, that i gave to you.

our engagement was bright, full of hopeful light,
but you couldn't handle what felt so right.
your hands were shaking, yet you still let go—
suddenly a stranger that i didn't know.

you told me you'd never been loved so deep,
and what we had was something you'd keep.
the kollmanii sold, like an afterthought,
a sign of the love you apparently forgot.

and i'm still here, holding what we once knew,
the remnants of promises, broken in two.
the kollmanii gone, my heart left to mourn—
i thought you'd stay, but you left for a storm.

approaching late-decemeber
thankful you got two!

we're unpacking our life, a fresh start ahead,
boxes, memories, new threads to be spread.
i reach for a box, and my ring catches tight,
a snap of metal, and it's no longer alright.

you don't panic, you just laugh,
"you've got two rings, dear, the clover one's intact."
i smile and nod, what a lucky break!
you had gotten two rings, so the clover i take.

the one that broke was just a slip,
the love i have—it never dips.
the clover ring remains, steady and strong,
reminding me where i belong.

we move on. the house, our own,
with love and luck, the seeds that have grown.
the clover stays, with me every day,
your love on my finger, never fading away.

maybe it was an omen afterall

we unpacked our lives, put things in their place,
the moments ahead, spent filling our space.
but my ring caught, and snapped with a sound,
and in that instant, a fear spun around.

it was brief—just a fleeting sigh—
a thought that flashed, then passed me by.
was it an omen, a sign of some kind?
or was it the insecurities i was leaving behind?

i convinced myself to push it aside,
but inside, i think i sensed shifting tides.
maybe it was intuition, or maybe just fear,
but my fears had been soothed when you called me "dear"

we kept moving, a life full of play,
but i wonder if i missed any signs that day.
the clover remained, steady and true,
but i can't shake the feeling it was already ending for you...

late-december
christmas

christmas morning, two extra stockings!
the sight makes my heart soar!
the joy you both have brought to me,
i couldn't ask for more!

all of us, matching jammies,
stockings full of gifts.
the glee, the joy, we catch it all
every fleeting blip.

the best gift of all this year,
isn't under that tree.
god—that's cliche as fuck,
but really, you're all i need.

the children open their presents—
we both do too—
but really, the best part of christmas,
is cuddling up next to you.

pretty sure you left the elf...

christmas morning, stockings bright,
did i miss the signs again?
the joy we caught, the gifts we wrapped,
already slipping thin?

jammies matched, the tree stood tall,
the photos staged just right.
but had your gaze already drifted,
away from me that night?

the best gift wasn't wrapped in bows,
or under the sparkling tree.
see—fucking cliche as hell,
but it still meant everything to me.

the kids shrieked joy, the lights all gleamed,
but i held on too tight.
the best part of christmas, i thought, was us—
but had your love already taken flight?

dawn of a new year

the clock struck midnight, we only had one.
but i think we succeeded, in making it fun
we hung balloons, in a hammock of wrapping.
he pulled them down, jumping and laughing

we read him some books—we almost always did.
then watched our shows, and talked about the year ahead.
i'm so excited to start this new year,
planning our wedding—august 2026, my dear!

i know it's a while, but it gives us time to create,
the most perfect wedding designed by the fates.
i think it's comforting—you wanting to marry me *right then*—
that day we walked to that balcony, and all this began.

but i'm in no rush, i've said that from the start.
i want to plan it proper, but i promise you my heart.

i technically believe new year should start with the
spring equinox, so i later started my year again...

the clock struck midnight, we only had one.
but i didn't see clearly, what had already begun.
we hung up balloons, in a hammock of dreams.
you smiled and laughed, but i don't think it was what it seemed.

we read him some books—we always would do,
but these stories were ending, and i didn't have a clue.
we talked about plans, the dates, the year,
did you already know, you wouldn't actually be there?

all the excitement, deflated so fast,
like all those balloons—too thin to outlast.
i thought it was commitment, your instinct to rush.
but i think you knew—waiting would be too much.

i thought it was fate, the balcony's start—
and now wonder if you were already discarding my heart.

approaching late january
maybe this will help the pain...

you're having a surgery, definitely not your first
but i've had two similar so, i know it's one of the worst
anxiously awaiting, the text from the doctor
texting your cousin, "i'd be lost without her!"

you're in recovery, it all went to plan
the first thing you asked, was to hold ginny's hand.
i beam at the nurse, "yup, that's me!"
and she leads me back, to you waiting for me.

we stop for some snacks, you rattle a list.
exclaimed your excitement when i just got all of it
the following days, you said you felt so loved
the best partner ever, i really tried to go beyond and above.

just part of life, but then we got sick,
i'll take care of you both—
we'll get through anything, thin or thick.

you asked for me coming out of anesthesia...

you were having surgery, i waited alone.
had recovery plans and notes, pulled up on my phone.
texting your cousin, so grateful for reassurance,
having no idea, we were about to run out of endurance.

you woke up and asked for me—to hold my hand—
but then you let go faster than i. will. ever. understand.
the nurse beamed at me, and i beamed along—
still believing, i was where i belonged.

we stopped for snacks, i bought your whole list—
trying to freeze-frame little moments of bliss.
you said you felt loved, i clung to the praise—
not knowing our love would be reduced to a phase.

we got sick together, i cared without fear—
but you were already...not really here...

beginning of february
for my readers, who've undoubtedly experienced heartbreak at some
point,

so here's the thing, i need to say—
i think we need a break,
me? from love, so you? take pause,
for a bit on the left page.

it hit so abruptly, it was just over,
she scoffed when i was shocked,
the pain cut so fucking deep.
my love just kinda got lost...

this next chapter flows a little different—
shadows outweigh the heart...
so i left silence for you to write,
if the inspiration should spark.

you see, this story feels...
way too much....like a movie—
she went to the hospital, broke up through text, betrayal—
i never wanted a life so juicy!

at first her reasons were pretty vague,
i really internalized everything.
but as things really took a turn,
relief set in that it was ending.

so during the pauses, seek some reflection;
maybe jot a note or two.
know that you'll see love again,
and then my shadows will leave pause for you...
slowly healing,
-ginny

breathe in..
exhale..

...

the final chapter

...

in case you didn't see through your tears,
the space below is for you, my readers...

.... inhale. . . . .
. . . .
. . . .
. . . .
. . . .
. . . .
. . . .
. . . .
. . . .
. . . .
. . . .
. . . .
. . . .
. . . .
. . . .
. . . .
. . . .
. . . .
. . . .
. . . .
. . . .
. . . .
. . . .
. . . .
. . . .
. . . .
. . . .

early february
"i just want to focus on my son..."

i'm worried sick, but understand—no, that's not true
please—tell me how to fix this! please—tell me what to do!
but i can't even ask you, you said to give you space.
you called *him*—didn't talk to me first—what a slap in the face.

even then i say, okay. it's not about me or you.
you called *him* for your son—it even sounded *kinda* true.
of course this book is hindsight, of the things i didn't see.
so how very convenient—*fated* maybe—that you later posted
confessions for me to see!

not just yet, i'm skipping ahead here—let me slow things down.
i'm at home. you called the storm. for now: *crying is the theme
sound*
i check in on his health, sparingly, the boy i still love so fierce.
respecting your wishes to give you space—my god, the silence sears.

despite my efforts, *we* get worse—something i couldn't fathom.
i'm doing exactly what you asked—
....
....what the hell has happened?

early february
kollmanii

kept in light, a sacred gift,
offered as a vow.
loved you in a language your heart spoke
living things—they're gone now.
memory rare, rooted in soil,
a home carved out for growth,
nurtured with hope, not just the plant—
i guess...
i guess just sell my troth...

so relieved they're out of the hospital...

a week ago, i didn't know,
your departure was your last.
i thought for sure that you'd come home,
that you wouldn't do something so...rash.

you said you didn't feel comfortable,
your son loves who you allow.
acted like i'd turn it into a fight,
so you'll go to your cousin's house

you didn't though, but i didn't know–
you turned off your location.
you really ended a whole-ass engagement,
without a conversation or explanation.

next night, found out by chance,
had to remove my card...
imagine my surprise at the recent delivery,
not to your cousin's yard.

that's the point it started to sink in,
though i didn't have much proof.
something in my gut already knew,
let's all sing a round of, "oof."

i bet your guilt is what triggered,
the chaos that built from there.
the accusations, manipulation,
while texting me from...where?

....
....
....
....
....
....
....
....
....
....
....
....
....
....
....
....
....
....
....
....
....
....
....
....
....
....
....
....
....
....
....
....
....
....

mid-february
giving you a plant would have been better...

i have no words, at least not many
for how valentine's day went
i won't go into details, but,
by the end of the day, i was spent.

a month ago, i had these visions
of another plant for her,
actually every holiday, gifts planned—
valentine's day '26—was gonna be big sur.

plants are really special though,
they are kinda her "thing"
one i fell so in love with—
one that makes her feel seen.

i had a few, that were set aside,
in someone else's tent.
thriving and growing leaves,
waiting for the "when"

one silver-lining from it all—
that tiktok-tea-worthy day—
is a friend, i happened to meet,
that now i talk to every day.

late-february
it's a relief this time...

the silence from you...
is familiar somehow...
reminds me of summer...
when this just started out...

early-march
it really is getting ridiculous...

11—that's it...
just the one.
the number of seconds on the doorbell cam,
retrieving that possession for your son.

you made it out to be a whole big thing—
but really it was fast.
"no, i won't put it by the road.
to be mistaken and taken, as trash."

mid-march
intuitive readers know what's up...
she really called it down to the month...

i knew your soul, or thought i did,
the fleeting secrets...trauma...the things you thought you hid.
my soul knew, too, when you drew near.
our hearts would ignite, then you'd disappear.

a whispered warning filled the air—"she'll run. they always do."
soul on fire, driven by fate, so i ignored every clue.
a prophecy, in quiet tone, delivered to my tears.
hourglass flipped, the clock began...i begged to keep the years.

each warning sign, a flag unfurled, but summer's joy disguised.
i hung my flag in your room, ignoring all the signs.
the ghosting glances, sharp but brief, the fleeting panic in your stare,
lies by omission, i gave you permission, words unsaid hung in the air.

avoidant heart, in shadows deep, trauma i accepted.
"not alone, we'll heal together"—offer taken, then rejected.
so i built a fire, burning bright, hoping your choice would break the
chain.
escape the labyrinth of your mind—i drew the map... all in vain.

with your left hand, you drew me close, a tender touch, a whispered
plea.
while with the right, you sold my promises, discarded my trust so
carelessly.
you followed paths you knew so well, right down that old worn
track. and when you ran, hand-in-hand with him, you didn't even
glance back.

approaching late-march
it would have been easier for
you to just take your stuff....

you came again to grab some stuff—
left a lot...again
you said now you have enough?
so i have all these boxes to toss
before i can start "the end?"

weeks since i packed stuff away,
can't tell you all the specifics
but some of the things you left behind,
i find so. fucking. horrific.

what about his legos? christmas ornaments?
am i expected to reach out?
do you not care? is it a game?
at this point, both, no doubt.

you said toss it. why am i surprised?
you did the same to me.
it's concerning that you discard so quick—
i think perhaps you saved me!

early april
at least i know now...

i didn't respond to a text one day,
post-wreckage; nothing to say.
so she twisted our story onto a thread,
where i was cruel, and love was dead.

reduced me to names that scorched my skin,
while she curled up in the storm again.
a fleeting post, few hours at most,
but algorithms...confessions from a ghost.

i'm not the villain she portrayed—
i'm every vow that never swayed.
she may not read this—but the world just might.
and i'll move on—a new book, i will write.

-yoda

approaching late-april
things we would have shared

your cat peed on my bed—the night before you got him.
it was my fault—i left a bag—but boy, was i reminded!
of that time you shared—the first date with your storm—
and how he peed right on his lap!
omg do cats always know, all i could do was laugh.

remember the visions we used to see—of flowers, purple and yellow?
you'll never guess the colors that bloomed once my life started to
mellow.
easter morning—baskets lined up, so much laughter and fun!
but don't you think i didn't feel the weight of that missing one.

the other night, a silly movie—i watched it with the bigs.
i started to cry, but wiped my tears—sometimes, healing feels rigged.
i have a garden—like, in the literal sense. flowers, yes, and veggies too.
but now i think i need a rabbit fence. it sucks—you would've known
what to do.

little bonfires in the evenings, skateboards on the deck.
i put a dog gate by the stairs, but i worry the kids still might break
their necks.
so many moments, even still, i first think to share with you.
but to be betrayed by what you did, can't hurt worse than losing
what *you* blew.

late-april
mirrors shatter

she loved the way i lit the dark,
and mirrored back my every spark.
her praise came soft, her smile wide,
words i thought came from inside.

the mirror walls she held with care
began to shake, too much to bear.
she couldn't carry all that weight—
the image cracked and sealed our fate.

each shatter left me more aware—
that *she* was never really there.
just smoke, and glass, and sleight of hand,
a house of mirrors, built on sand.

she mirrored to me what i am,
desperately trying to uphold her sham.
she dressed in traits she saw in me,
then blamed *me* when she couldn't be.

and when the final trick was done,
she dropped the mask—she chose to run.
i watched her fade, a disappearing act—
a hollow frame, a heart that lacks.

but from the mess, i cut the thread—
i found the "me" i thought was dead.
and stitched my tapestry with seams of gold—
less shadows now...more love to hold.

...exhale....

late april
i found someone...

thoughts of you in my head, running through nonstop
but not in the ways, of those first days, more in a way of naught.
your love replaced, by someone else—i think you may have met her.
she goes by "ginny" in most crowds, though your memory may be a
bit blurred.

whispers of love, betrayal, and silence, loop around as she creates:
the gift that she had planned for you—but a little different, with a
twist of fate.
see, here's the thing, there are no regrets, for not a single minute.
she loved you hard, dreamt of your lives, but what did she gain,
without you in it?

a home, she never would have found, had not for her commitment.
exactly what she'd always dreamed, aside from *you* not in it.
a space that fulfills in ways others can't—once shared—'til *you*
brought chaos in.
souls she wouldn't have otherwise known—she even gets to play her
the guitar again.

a friend you probably would have loved—though paths would have
never crossed,
had you not pushed the boundaries—threatened to break her
locks....
so no regrets, there's truly not.
well, she can only speak for herself—
she can't imagine making someone else their entire world,
then burning it all down, in your storm of hell.

good luck, babe! i bet you notice now ;-)
...maybe the shadows aren't completely gone yet...

did you ever notice,
the things that slipped between the cracks?
ice water waiting every night—
even when you'd turn your back?

i knew the wants you used to hide,
before you even formed the thought.
microexpressions—i paid attention.
i knew the things you never sought.

you didn't need to ask—i knew.
the little things you didn't say.
oh, the things i had planned for you—
you have no idea the life you threw away!

now, i wonder if they've died,
the quiet parts that i kept warm...
to trade for—what exactly?
you gave up peace for a thunderstorm!

do you even miss them now?
the little things that never spoke?
or did you forget them when you burned us down—
a victim lost in your maze of smoke?

do they hit you, or just drift by—
thoughts of the home that you gave up?
does he even know you want ice in your water?
because all i've got left is... "babe, good luck!"

late april
"shadows of a journal"....coming soon!

she'll see my name and tilt her head,
"it can't be," she'll think instead.
but page by page, the words will glow—
and god, she'll feel what she let go.

no paperback to catch the storm's eye,
no cover obscured, where truth might lie.
she'll buy the kindle, dim the screen—
compelled to feel guilt in every. scene.

she'll recognize, the words unsaid,
the soft confessions, the puzzles spread.
and memories she thought were small—
she'll see i remembered, she'll read them all.

but really these words, they aren't for her,
some once were, but now it's more obscure.
i'm writing for healing—though—
she deserves to know how much she was loved,
maliced? nah, but you decide: see the line above.

late april
i hope you brought an umbrella...

it appears i blame the storm a lot,
but i promise you, i swear i'm not.
for storms will come, and storms will go—
but it's a choice to leave your home.

thunderstorms are opportunists—
don't care about boundaries.
that was something that *she* broke:
the vows between her and me.

she knew what it could lead to,
but justified it in her head.
at times probably regretted it—
but i would have forgiven up until his bed.

one of the lyrics, she tried to spin,
is we didn't share the things we liked.
here's a line shared-interests translate:
the storm was the getaway car—am i right?!

late april
sometimes love bleeds into shadows
to clear the storms...

"are the plants okay?"
"yeah, what's the worry?"
me sending a video of plants standing in glory

narratives spin, tornadoes sweep through—
apparently having no idea just how many,
conversations we'd had about you.

not about *this*—spilling tea *wasn't* my thing—
plants, plants, plants, *more plants*—
like the one i gave you with your ring!

so that's one person that didn't think your new script fit—
i gave my side—but kept it vague—
but he had already seen beyond it.

i don't understand all the bridges you lit—a plant connection?? come
on.
ooohhh–it's 'cause you had him sell my gift!
well, now i just feel dumb...

that makes more sense—it just came to me—
i externally process—
something i've learned about myself in therapy.

thank you for that—helping me realize—
i was losing myself
long before you said goodbye.
(continues on next page)

having her support though,
those days after you left—
changed the way grief could have settled into my chest.

i gave her part of my book—shit's getting real.
it's going to be published,
and it's going to make people *feel*

they'll feel the tiny sparks of hope, through early journal days.
first written before we even met in person...
in this lifetime, anyway...

they'll feel the sting of "just friends," probably like *i* did
having shadows they can't ignore—
looming right there like *he* did.

they'll read our love story, already mourning.
seeing love that was real but—
sort of already knowing the ending of the story...

every love poem written—from summer to now—
was real—
but now they echo like fading sounds.

love poems hit different, when you see the hindsight.
but it was the string bean poem
that really pulled everything in tight.

every page of my journal, just out there for all to read.
but i'm manifesting a best-seller—
something great from this grief.
(continues on next page)

and my real journal pages weren't written in rhymes,
except for the poems, of course,
that were written in real-time.

but the journal was the blueprint—for every detail written within—
from the moment my soul recognized yours,
and my love to started to leak in.

i know that sounds all "woo-woo"
but it's what i still believe.
"fated connections" just don't always mean "partners of destiny"

when i was building our life, each day was chosen.
were you planning to run,
or was it a spur of the moment?

i often wonder if you have regrets—looking back, i don't.
i stuck with my integrity then—
and now in the words i wrote.

do i wish i hadn't yelled, when you invaded my space?
of course! but my therapist assured me was normal—
she literally heard it during my appointment taking place.

never once did i threaten, never once did i beg.
i respected every boundary i could,
while you ran, twisted, and hid.

based on psychology, i'm betting you're still putting on a show.
you left for "true loves kiss"
isn't that how that line goes?
(continues on next page)

mid-august will be tougher for you, our anniversary of that kiss.
one i never would have initiated first—
because i respect boundaries and all that shit.

"i just hope you don't get hurt"—kindness from a friend,
it just might be worth it
and so i let it begin.

and if my soul could do it all over, even knowing how it'd end.
i'd hit redo and replay the script
exactly the same way again.

at this point in my journey, i know it was necessary—
(let me know if you guys want merch)
no, no, i joke...though...*that would be legendary...*
(continues–just kidding)

late april
4-leaf clovers

i still find clovers,
all over my yard.
confirmation of the things,
i gained on "hard."

reliving all these memories...
has shown me i'm not broken.
i love hard. i love pure.
even when i'm jokin'.

i'm funny, kind, really dorky,
though, that's just my observation...
and when i'm not trying so hard,
things will manifest into creation.

i'll no longer accept crumbs,
where there should be a meal.
no longer play the games,
of someone afraid to feel.

i have golden retriever energy—
was maybe a tad naive.
black cat energy matched me well—
just not the cat and mouse and leave.

i didn't come this far, to only come this far—
my journey has just begun,
i'll pay attention to how the next one starts...
no more getaway cars, hun. ;-)

late april
weekend novelty

a new shredder, nothing remarkable
but why'd it bring up memories of that carnival?
i think it's the way the laugher sounds,
missing an echo of what once was found.

the garden waits, the earth is kind,
it'll grow from ghosts you left behind.
it all takes time, the best things do,
compost... healing... forgetting you...

i watch kids spin, i hear them roar—
the life we could have shared and more.
and though the joy rings softer, bare—
the echos are loud enough to fill the air.

you left the dreams you could not keep.
so i plant them deep. i let them seep.
in the gardens you'll never see—
i continue the life you chose to flee.

you left the dreams we swore were ours,
but i return them to the flowers.
even storms get their day—
to feed new seeds of power.

but i do not burn what we became.
i plant it deep—new growth from pain.
and in the gardens she won't see,
i'll grow the life she swore was me.

late april
end of an era (see what i did there?)

i could keep writing, but i think i've learned now:
the capacity of my love, and what i'll allow.
these poems, these memories, i held them true—
but now i wrap up the story you blew.

so many more memories, i had to leave out—
a short time in love, but i had no doubts.
there was so much more laugher, jokes, and joy.
details mundane, but i was writing *our story.*

i think in rhymes now, i'm writing so often—
the words flowing out of me, nails in this coffin.
as i lay down my phone, close google docs:
i hereby seal this vault, closed with a lock.

late april
thank you for going along
on this journey with me

i'm sitting here in awe, at what i've just finished—
encapsulated a part of my life, instead of letting it diminish.

do you know how much fun it is, to tell stories with rhymes?
it makes me want to do another—a new story, for another time.

i've always said my life felt like a movie, but maybe it's really a book.
that actually makes way more sense, now that i take another look.

maybe not just one, but two, or three, or four—
hell, this one only covered a year, but it sure as hell felt like more.

reflecting on all that i've survived, this wasn't even my worst.
devastating? yes. heart-wrenching? yup. but i'm working through the hurt.

i took the love i had, and turned it into art—
a journey into my journal, a journey into my heart.

love doesn't disappear overnight, but it can be redirected.
left alone, inside and dry, i found more than i expected.

in love, peace, and growth
-ginny

....
....
....
....
....
....
....
....
....
....
....
....
....
....
....
....
....
....
....
....
....
....
....
....
....
....
....
....
....
....
....*exhale*....

here's some space for you...to breathe. . . . .
. . . . *inhale.* . . . .
. . . .
. . . .
. . . .
. . . .
. . . .
. . . .
. . . .
. . . .
. . . .
. . . .
. . . .
. . . .
. . . .
. . . .
. . . .
. . . .
. . . .
. . . .
. . . .
. . . .
. . . .
. . . .
. . . .
. . . .
. . . .
. . . .
. . . .
. . . .
. . . .

....
....
....
....
....
....
....
....
....
....
....
....
....
....
....
....
....
....
....
....
....
....
....
....
....
....
....
....
....
....
....
....
....*exhale...*

.... *inhale.* ....
....
....
....
....
....
....
....
....
....
....
....
....
....
....
....
....
....
....
....
....
....
....
....
....
....
....
....
....
....
....
....
....

. . . .
. . . .
. . . .
. . . .
. . . .
. . . .
. . . .
. . . .
. . . .
. . . .
. . . .
. . . .
. . . .
. . . .
. . . .
. . . .
. . . .
. . . .
. . . .
. . . .
. . . .
. . . .
. . . .
. . . .
. . . .
. . . .
. . . .
. . . .
. . . .
. . . .
. . . .
. . . . *exhale* . . . .

.... *inhale.* ....
....
....
....
....
....
....
....
....
....
....
....
....
....
....
....
....
....
....
....
....
....
....
....
....
....
....
....
....
....
....
....
....
....
....

....
....
....
....
....
....
....
....
....
....
....
....
....
....
....
....
....
....
....
....
....
....
....
....
....
....
....
....
....
....
....*exhale*....